Two Lemons and Five Lumps of Sugar

A wartime saga of five and a half years

Marjorie Prior

Dedication to "Two lemons and Five Lumps of Sugar"

I dedicate this book to the memory of my husband Fred Prior, Principal Probation Officer of Hull who died suddenly in February 1971.

To my four children Catherine, Melanie, Alison and Julian. To my nine grandchildren, Emily, Chris, Kathleen, Edwin, Joshua, Alec, Aimée, Matthew and Ben. I dedicate this finally to my late father Joseph Wood Matthews whose experience in France in the 1st World War led to this story.

Contents

Preface:-		5
Chapter 1	The journey starts	7
Chapter 2	The Family	11
Chapter 3	The Shrine	14
Chapter 4	The First Month	16
Chapter 5	Late Summer of 1940, Part 1	21
	Part 2	27
Chapter 6	The Farm Girl	30
Chapter 7	Two lemons and five lumps of sugar	33
Chapter 8	The Precious Tongue	36
Chapter 9	1944 - My 5th year	38
Chapter 10	The beginning of The End	41
Chapter 11	The End	47

Preface

As a child school was the centre of my life. I loved it, loved reading, loved drawing, loved sport, accepted the discipline (although a chatterbox!) and worked hard.

My parents encouraged me. On a Saturday afternoon, home from work, my father would spend an hour with me on his lap translating a children's story from a French newspaper that he had bought on the way home from work. We lived in East Croydon and he took the suburban line from Central London each day. He had become interested in French because of his war time experiences in France, (1914-1918 War) where as a sapper he spent time in Ypres, Arras and other front line localities. We still have some of his letters sent to my mother at that time, written in beautiful copper plate writing in indelible pencil.

I can remember the great Crystal Palace fire. One Monday evening 30th November 1936, coming out of my Youth Club we noticed a bright glow spreading over the southern sky. What could this be? A massive fire somewhere, but in the flat valley we could see nothing. Where could we get a good view? — on Shirley Hills! We bolted up Shirley Road and on to the undulating hills beyond the houses. Having reached the flat top we stopped. The complete valley lay below us and on the skyline between our hill and London we saw a glowing mass. A brilliant spectacle of burning glass was flaming in the wind. As we watched one of the huge towers called a 'pepper pot' started toppling over as would a gigantic rocket, with sparks darting from it like an enormous flaring firework.

We could hear nothing, but saw the burning of this Victorian crystal glass palace, whipped up by the wind, that I had once visited as a little girl in the 1920's.

Three years later, too young to go to college at 17 my school suggested that it would be a good idea for me to have the experience of an 'au pair' student in France. My French teacher knew of a family of two Head teachers in Morlaix, Finistere. I was to go at the end of the school year and return a year later to attend Avery Hill Training College for an Infants course of 3 years. Little did I know that my year abroad would develop into five and a half years. In other words I would spend more than a quarter of my life absorbing and imbibing French in a country where 'perfide albion' had not been forgotten!

"You're alright" said a certain older son of the family to me one day — but the others ...."!

"I wish I liked the Human Race
I wish I liked its silly face
And when I'm introduced to one
I wish I thought - what jolly fun!
This book is part witness.

CHAPTER 1

The Adventure Starts

On Wednesday July 21st 1939 I left E. Croydon station with my school French teacher and a large blue trunk to travel to the boat train, Dover-Calais and then on to Paris. My teacher was going on to some friends of hers. She was going to put me on to the right train in Paris to take me down to Dijon in the Côte d'Or, where I had been told that the French family spent their summer holidays. I was to take care of the two younger children of a Headmaster and Headmistress, first during the holidays and then after at school in Morlaix.

I remember noticing in the boat with great interest a family of four, mother French, father English and two little girls aged about four and six. Mother spoke to them always in French, Father always in English, the girls spoke to Mother in French, to Father in English, to one another in either French or English. Father appeared to use French to his wife. Confusing perhaps to an outsider, but not to the family itself.

I was going to the holiday home of a Headmaster and Headmistress whom I understood had quite a large family. It was the summer holiday in Central France. The family lived and worked in Morlaix in Brittany.

In Paris I had my first French breakfast — a bowl of drinking chocolate and a roll, at 6.30 am, at a table outside a restaurant near to the station; and it was different — the smell, the sounds — the voices of course. I have never ceased to feel that difference, the hundreds of times I have been to France since 1939. The thought of a warm morning in a French cobbled inner courtyard of their many, many blocks of flats conjures up the smell of 'fougeres' — fern dampened by early dew or freshly watered by various tenants, clicking open their wooden shutters against the grey walls and calling out the morning greetings to their neighbours while throwing over the balcony rail their airing bed clothes.

However, I caught my French fast train to Dijon where I understood I was to be met by a Monsieur Schlemmer. In the carriage a young French man spotting my luggage and no doubt my Englishness — anxious to try out **his** English language, engaged me in conversation and promised to help me find Monsieur le Principal who was meeting me at 11 am. We arrived. The train emptied and so did the platform. No one was left except a stray porter or two. The young man walked me to the barrier waited a further ten minutes looking this way and that and finally, apologising, left me at the Station Master's office. The Station Master was obviously not used to being left with a 17 year old young English lady with heavy suitcases and hesitant bookish French tried asking me in rapid local speech — who? where? … It wasn't until I wrote down the name of my Monsieur … Schlemmer (a German name actually and I was pronouncing it "Schlemma") and the name of the village where the summer holiday was spent, that the penny dropped. All smiles he picked up his telephone (he wound it up!) and 'phoned the village postmaster (who possessed the **only** 'phone in the village) who rushed down the lane and informed Monsieur Schlemmer in the big house that an English demoiselle was waiting at Dijon station — that another penny dropped! Dear Papa remembered he had got his dates mixed up and that he was supposed to meet me on that Thursday morning at Dijon. The village Beaumont sur Vingeanne was a good 30 miles away!!

By this time I was very hungry (having last eaten at 6.30 in the morning — my sparse French breakfast!) felt grubby and dishevelled, overdressed in travelling clothes, and just beginning to have a sinking feeling of being lost and almost abandoned. I had been on holidays in England without parents but at least I could talk and explain if in a predicament! This time I had the language problem — was I saying the right thing in the right way and I remembered the silly story of the polite Chinese missionary who not realising that Chinese was a tonal language insulted a gentleman by referring to his wife as a donkey instead of a beautiful lady — or some similar bad mistake!

At about 4 o'clock I was waiting in the Station Master's office (no luxury apartment) — trains outside coming and going as was the man himself, the door burst open and a man dashed up to me "Mademoiselle Marrjoree Mattevs — profuse apologies — smiles all around especially from the Station Master — feelings of tremendous relief from me — I was found!!

A large rosy faced teenage girl was introduced to me — Françoise — there were only 3 months between us — she was to accompany me while Monsieur saw to my luggage, and off we went on foot. I was hungry, really hungry. It was hot. I was overdressed. Within minutes I stuttered to Françoise that I was very thirsty and hungry and immediately she conveyed to Monsieur this fact, though she called him Uncle Henri **not** Papa — the explanation of this family mystery was revealed to me later.

We hurried along to a big open French restaurant where I was given a large bowl of chocolate and 2 flakey French croissants — very gratefully received by me — before going to a bus station where amongst much clatter and shouting were loaded on to a small village bus, my trunk, several crates of fresh peaches, several bulky passengers and hot red faced Papa, tired plump Françoise and overdressed me.

We bumped and rattled along on uncomfortable wooden seats, stopping at several villages with much clatter and chatter and unloading and remounting. Late afternoon the driver/conductor shouted out "Beaumont sur Vingeanne next stop". More bustle hustle and chatter. Hot overdressed me (I believe I was even wearing stockings!) got out of the bus, luggage was unloaded, people were met, crates were piled up, villagers stared, I could smell farms and cows. We were accompanied down the short uneven dry rutted lane by the postmaster Isidore a small crowd of inquisitive villagers viewing with curiosity this "Mademoiselle L' Anglaise" who was coming to the Laguilhaumme - Schlemmer household — the said household with 11 children, already a good talking point in the locality. A village of 126 souls consisting of only 4 main families and various smaller fry, knows everybody's business, and what it doesn't know it makes up! What I learnt about the intimate lives of many of the village folk defies description and would fill another book.

So hot, dishevelled, tired but excited I was taken into the 'big house' via a forbidding heavy iron gate through 2 small courtyards and up some inner wooden stairs across sloping floors to a high charming little balcony room overlooking the most glorious countryside. I was left alone having been shown the quite primitive washing facilities and told that the evening meal would be at 7.30 pm.

My unknown adventures had begun.

Chapter 2

The Family

The following days (end of July and August 1939) were spent in a gentle whirlwind — mildly bewildering! — falling into a routine completely unknown to me, living within this large family, eating different foods meeting different people.

The house was a mini-chateau, over 150 years old with a prominence of stone floors, walls, staircases and a turret. The 'best' rooms had parquet floors and draped material on the walls often with matching curtains — the minor rooms were of stone and irregularly shaped. All had wooden shutters opening outwards with smaller windows opening inwards, folding into the side walls on larger rooms. The turret was used by tiny bats who swooped in and out in the summer evenings.

The days were spent looking after the two younger children Jacques 3, Yette $1^{1}/_{2}$ (I was shown the pattern of their day by Emma the eldest daughter aged 24) and the evenings were spent walking in the country lanes singing in chorus the many songs they all knew and learnt from one another. On the rare occasions when it rained (it never seemed to that summer) we spent indoors chatting and planning but **never** with the parents. I listened — tried to understand — the lower the tone the more private was the conversation! The parents were in the large elegant 'salon'. Maman, the headmistress knitting, always something for Jacques or Yette, and Papa reading or discussing serious matters with her.

At a given time we would troop into the salon to say goodnight. Each offspring in turn kissing each parent on each cheek "Bonsoir Maman, kiss kiss Bonsoir Uncle Henri kiss kiss or Bonsoir Papa kiss kiss Bonsoir Tante Juliette kiss kiss. This nightly ceremony staggered me — my two little ones were long gone to bed, but there were nine left, and there were Uncles and Aunts as well as Mums and Dads. I needed an explanation and within two or three days, Emma the eldest daughter seized a quiet moment and attempted to explain the family situation.

Monsieur Schlemmer had been married but his wife died leaving him with three children, Emma, René and Riquet (Henri). Madame Schlemmer had been married to a Monsieur Laguilhaumie who died leaving her with six children, Jean, Françoise, Claude Monique Noel and Philippe. She was posted to a large girls' school in Morlaix, Finistere. He was posted also to the large boys' school in Morlaix. They met and married and had two children — my Jacques and Yette — so 3 plus 6 made 9 plus 2 made 11!!

If, dear Reader, you think this is complicated, add to it two other problems. In the French language there are two words for "you," 'tu' and 'vous'. One is for family and small children — or occasionally derision — the other for adults, strangers and general conversation. Which one was I to use remembering there were 11 plus 2 parents? To complicate matters there were both a Mum and Dad and an Aunt and Uncle for every child except my two little ones who only had a straight forward Mother and Father. If I wanted to give a message to Monique (aged 13) for example from her **mother** I would say "Maman would like you to … ….:" but if it were from Monsieur I would say "Uncle Henry would like you to … …." but on the other hand if I needed to give a message to Riquet aged 11 from Madame, I would have to say "Tante Juliette wants you to … … " or if from his father

"Papa wants you to ... ...". Complicated?? — add these two problems together — the tu and vous and the Maman and Tante and in what for me was a foreign language you can appreciate that my first few months in France were enlightening to say the least.

Chapter 3

The Shrine

About 2 miles from our house at Beaumont was a large old rambling building in spacious grounds owned by an elderly couple. From them we could buy quantities of fresh vegetables and any fruits that were in season. They loved being visited by us all, and off we went one afternoon pulling with us two small hand-carts containing baskets and sacks for our possible purchases — we never quite knew what they would have for us in season. The youngest children were riding in the little carts, we older ones were singing and laughing along the country lanes — there was no traffic at that time of day.

On arrival, having introduced me as an extra to our large family, Françoise (at 17 being the oldest was in charge) said how many lettuces, new potatoes, carrots and leeks (if they had them) we should like. Certain lettuces are cooked as a vegetable in France so to order 40 of these was not an exorbitant amount. While the elderly couple were busying themselves picking and pulling the fresh vegetables we were told to help ourselves to any of the ripe fruits in the orchard, especially the cherries. Never had I seen such a cherry tree! Almost as tall as a small elm it was still covered in enormous red juice cherries right down to the ground! We lay on our backs on the warm grass holding the dipping thin branches, and literally plucked the cherries from their stalks with our mouths, spitting the stones out sideways, giggling all the while. Struggling to our feet after 20 minutes of this activity we wandered over to our dear elderly host and hostess.

They smiled at us and then hesitatingly pausing a moment pointed out what appeared to be a tiny stone house by itself in the middle of the garden. "As you have become friends of ours", the lady said, "we should like to show you our tiny chapel," and they led us to the small stone house.

Unlocking the door she went in. We followed her into a tiny room. It was a little girl's paradise! The ceiling and walls were covered in pictures, children's pictures. Dainty curtains were pulled over the little windows. Bright soft rugs were on the floor. Stuffed animals and dolls of all sizes covered the small bed and every spare space. We were amazed. The elderly lady spoke,. "We had a daughter who died when she was thirteen, and this is her room. We threw nothing away, I keep her room clean every week, put fresh sheets on the bed, so you see she is still with us."

We withdrew from this dear little house into the large tended garden. We paid our bill and thoughtfully tramped home, with our freshly picked fruit and vegetables.

I have never forgotten this dear couple, and over the many years since, and in the company of laughing children in other cherry orchards have reflected that we weathered adults should perhaps count our blessings and not feel sorry for ourselves.

Chapter 4

The First Month, August 1939

Hot, sweet smelling mornings, with a mist rising from flat meadows visible from my bedroom window, with a stream filtering through willow trees — these were my first impressions of France in the summer of 1939. Slowly the house would wake up, nobody in a hurry. Maids in the kitchen (just below me) would be talking in hushed voices, already preparing the midday meal for at least sixteen people. What was I supposed to do? Wash and dress? Where? There was a little table in my room with a jug and basin on it. I used them, thinking rapidly where was the apology for a toilet that I had been shown the evening before. I had to leave my room, go through a large low ceilinged bedroom occupied by 3 boys to another door. This led into a rickety little passage (the floor tiles clicked) across a very dry wide boarded loft where in the corner behind a door was a W.C. This did resemble a little an English town version.

(One of these days I am going to produce a book called 'Continental toilets I have known'. Townsfolk I have met both in England and France find it hard to believe!)

The new faces, the new patterns of the day, the continual chatter, laughter and grumbles, the totally different atmosphere, began to fall into some sort of shape. I gathered that the family were used to having a young lady from abroad, preferably English as a nursery assistant and companion and tutor for the older girls. The two parents were at work all day and a cook, Marie, and maids, did all the housework.

The little ones were amenable. Their French at $1\frac{1}{2}$ and 3 years old was as good as mine! and I absorbed it along with them; but very, very soon I learnt what an authoritarian father and mother could be like. If I wanted to be happy in my job I had to grasp this and adapt accordingly.

I remember clearly one evening in the 'Salon' where I was sitting quietly winding down, out of the blue a strident voice was heard approaching and Papa entered quickly. (A rapid entry is much noisier on bare wood parquet flooring). A face to face encounter was brewing between Father and eldest daughter Emma, who would have been nearly 25. "For as long as you are under my roof you'll do as I say" he nearly spat it out. She attempted a reply. He cut her dead "Be quiet" he said, "and leave the room!". No wonder a few months later my little Jacques popped his face round the playroom door one morning and said slowly in his little boy's French "Is Papa in a good mood this morning?" He had already suffered the strident slings and arrows of his father, and Jacques was only 3!

Within two days Emma took the opportunity to explain to me the slight complications of this large family of eleven children. As I have already mentioned both parents had married before, both partners had died and both had remarried. Monsieur had had 3 children, 1 daughter and two sons, Emma was **his** eldest daughter. Madame had had 6 children, three daughters and three sons, Jean was **her** eldest son. Jacques and Yette were **their** children making in all 11 children ages ranging from 25 to $1\frac{1}{2}$ yrs.

Complications were inbuilt because of the mixed relationships, and the very nature of the French language itself, Monsieur's three children called him Papa and used the French 'tu' (thou) when speaking to him — but called Madame, Tante Juliette and used 'vous' (you) to her. On the other hand Madame's six children used the French 'tu' (thou) to her called her naturally Maman and called him Onde Henry and used 'vous' when speaking to him!

But of course for the two youngest Jacques and Yette the situation was different. Monsieur and Madame were naturally Papa and Maman and 'tu' to both! To complicate matters in French the word 'you' is automatically 'vous' if applied to more than one person — the little ones said 'tu' to all their older half-sisters and brothers. At first I was 'Mademoiselle' to all and the word 'vous' for you was politely used, showing to outsiders that I was not related to any of the family. But a strange thing happened. Over the months and the political events, the external ongoings altered our relationships and I became 'tu' not 'vous' to all except the parents the two eldest children and the maids. The children maintained their original surnames so that we had 6 Laguilhaumie (Mother's side) 3 Schlemmers (Father's side) and the two little Schlemmers (Mother's and Father's second marriage children).

So after 2 or 3 months I became used to saying to Riquet "Run and ask Tante Juliette if she wants you to wear your blue trousers today and ask Papa if he said be ready by two or half past two"; or to Noël (Madame's son) "Run and ask Maman if she wants you to wear your black trousers and ask Uncle Henri if he said you needed such and such a thing"!!

This was not exactly what a 17 year old girl learnt at school if she learnt any spoken French at all! In school we would have studied some of the classics, some formal French expressions and some French poetry but not many little homely expressions that are needed in every day speech in a family with small children.

...... This large family became even more complicated. Three years later (in the middle of the war) Emma Schlemmer (Monsieur's eldest daughter) married Jean Laguilhaumie (Madame's eldest son). They were no blood relation whatsoever and they had a family — five children, four girls and a boy, Catherine, Jacqueline, Jean-Mi, Anne and Martine. These children of course only had two grandparents, my original Maman and Papa Schlemmer.

After I returned to England (as the 'doodlebugs' were perfecting themselves before VE Day) I was nearly killed by a 'rocket' that fell in the centre of the meat market in Farringdon Rd London in the middle of the morning. There was no warning and the deaths and destruction were appalling. It would have been ironic to have survived the German occupation in France only to have 'come home' and be killed in London!

Weather-wise August 1939 was beautiful but I sensed straight away in the village, people were disquieted, chatting in groups and talking of War. My father not usually an optimist in this subject having been in the trenches in France during the first World War, wrote to me to stay with the family. Very suddenly the administrative machine of France pulled out the plug — headmasters and mistresses were called back as civil servants to their posts and at the end of August we had to move — 11 children, two parents, 4 maids and me to return to the large school in Morlaix where the family had a flat. The home journey was long. Back to the town of Dijon — I remember eating choucroûte in a restaurant crowded and noisy. All of us loaded with bags and cases, trying to find seats on a main line train to Paris and changing to another long distance train to take us to Morlaix in Finistere — miles and miles, (at least kilometres and kilometres!) We were all bedraggled and hot and thirsty — tired but not frightened.

We arrived in the morning. Somehow we put small children to bed, attempted to settle, and looked after one another. Maman and Papa immediately had to busy themselves with school problems and the maids and cook had to see to meals as well as being worried about **their** families (brothers and fathers) who would be called up. On September 1st 1939 I remember hearing the sirens sound for general mobilisation — every man knew where he had to report to and we could see in the streets below our flat people hurrying and bustling, reporting to the appropriate place.

On September 3rd War was declared and Neville Chamberlain made his famous speech. The 'phoney war' had begun.

Chapter 5

Late Summer 1940

Part 1

The Germans (les Boches) came down the sloping road on the eastern side of Morlaix, tanks, lorries, infantry — a long file of foreign uniforms — into the town centre. It was the 19th June 1940, I was living in the large school on the opposite side of the valley and we waited to see what would happen. The town was horribly silent, no traffic was about. The soldiers were billeted in the French army barracks, French speaking Germans took over the Administration which became the Commissariat and within a few days Papa informed me that I was required to report to a local office. All foreign nationals, as always, were registered in France, rather like our old library ticket system and it would have been a simple matter to flick through the cards in strict alphabetical order to find my name and address.

I found the office, knocked on the door, "entrez" was shouted in hesitant French, and I met Herr Bauer — a balding, kindly, gentle German soldier about the age of my own father, who beckoned me over. In halting French he told me that he was an army clerk had a daughter eighteen (my age) at home, and quietly said that he hoped the War would end soon! I was required to sign on at that office every day — so every day I did, sometimes taking with me my two small French charges as part of their morning walk. French shopkeepers began to perk up with an increase in trade and German soldiers very politely, with heel clicking salutes of "Heil Hitler", bought, to the shopkeepers amazement, entire shelves of stockings and underclothes, needles and thread, to send back to their families in Germany. Much later I realised that Hitler's phrase "Guns before Butter" had meant precisely that. German soldiers in groups would invade the many restaurants and cafés and order enormous quantities of food. (Brittany was the market garden of France with fresh butter and artichokes a speciality). An omelette of twelve eggs was not unusual — and by going outside in the street to relieve themselves of an over-full stomach — they would return to the restaurant and start again. They always paid and were much more honest and polite than the previous English Tommies! The French shopkeepers who knew me well as "l'Anglaise au college" informed me of this — an indignity that I had to suffer with a weak smile and an apology!!

    The French school term was ending. The 14th July annual festivities were in abeyance — my French family's usual exit to the country was delayed — Emma was entrapped in Rennes where her University had closed down, the eldest son Jean was of enlisting age and his whereabouts was unknown. The unreliable news bulletins reported 3 million French prisoners. Unexpected news was suddenly thrust upon us. One morning as I was with Jacques and Yette in their nursery, one of the French maids we called Ninani came hurriedly into the play room and said "Madame and Monsieur want to see you immediately in the 'salon'. I'll look after the little ones." This was most unusual at 10 o'clock in the morning! I hurried along the wide corridor of our flat and went into the salon. Monsieur and Madame Schlemmer were standing there looking very serious. I stopped short wondering why I had been called. "Bam Bam" said Monsieur, "Listen carefully. What would you say if I told you that this afternoon the Germans were coming here to collect you." He paused. "What would I say?" I said to myself "I'd never been asked such a question before" — nor had met any unpleasant Germans. "I suppose" I replied, "it would be a new experience for me." He was dumbfounded. He never forgot that answer, and years later after the war when meeting him in totally different circumstances he reminded me of it. His recollection of his meeting with Germans as a young man in 1914 when he had had to hide his identity and actually became a spy for the French, where the German invasion of France in Alsace/Lorraine was so different, had coloured completely his idea of what my reaction would be!

So he simply said, "Right — pack a large bag with warm clothes" — Madame interrupted saying "she'd better take a pair of your winter pyjamas" — "your washing necessities; have a good lunch with the rest of us as usual and be ready to leave at 1.50 pm. Ninani can look after the little ones — I will accompany you and promise you that on no condition will I allow the Germans to leave with you alone!"

I can see the whole scene as clearly as though it were yesterday. At 2pm promptly, the front door bell was rung (a very loud sounding one on the ground floor) a German Officer presented himself — Papa spoke quickly and firmly to him — I was waved out — down the steps, the two men following me, and was ushered into the back seat of a large black cab. I saw a youngish nun in black and white. She burst into tears immediately on seeing me. "Oh" she cried in English "what will become of us?" "Well nothing at the moment' I replied practically, "Let's see where we are going first." Monsieur, the German Officer and a driver (I don't know whether he was

French or German but he seemed to know the way) spoke quietly and we two in the back appeared to be free to speak to one another.

Sister Madelaine (as I found out on asking) was a young Canadian nun, on a visit to her Order in France when War broke out, did not or could not return and had been picked up unexpectedly by the Germans because she was of Canadian descent. What damage she could or would have done I do not know. An over zealous German Officer was carrying out orders, but knowing now just what some incredible nuns **did** do during the War he was perhaps wise.

After some time bumping along on country roads we came to a small town on this summer afternoon in August and stopped. People took little interest in us. Papa was talking to the German and gave me a reassuring look. We got out, entered a building, traipsed up some narrow dark stairs on to a first floor corridor — lit only by sunlight coming through one or two wooden doors opening from small rooms. We stopped. I looked in to see a very young girl in a nun's brown habit and bare footed washing the floor. It appeared tidy. Papa told her gently to pack up her things and go. A small clean room with a bed complete with sheets a chair and little else, confronted me. Papa turned to the German pointed to the door handle and said, "This door has no lock on it. I am <u>not</u> leaving an 18 year old young lady by herself under such circumstances." The German hesitated, some rapid speech passed between them and before I knew what was happening, a local locksmith had been called and was fitting on the inside of the door a firm lock and bolt so that the door could be secured from the inside.

"I've got to go now," said Monsieur, but looking me straight in the eyes, "you are never to go into your room without bolting the door firmly behind you. Do you understand? And when you leave — lock it and take the key with you."

He left on promising to return the next day. It was midsummer. The weather was hot. I could hear sounds, quiet talking everywhere. I needed to find out who else was in this odd place. I could hear children's and women's voices, some English but mostly French. I looked out of the window onto a dusty courtyard with some rough looking huts, a pump and small lavoir and people moving around. Was food provided or what? I would go and see.

I went down the dark staircase, through a kind of scullery out into the sunshine and stopped a young woman, who appeared to be about my age. "Excuse me, are you French or English". "I'm English" she said "but I want to be a French nun in a closed Order and the silly Germans took me out of it and put me here!"

She took me into one of the large huts which was busy with women and children attempting to make some sort of order out of chaos and give themselves some family privacy by tying up wires or ropes between windows across the hut to make screens. I was aware of one or two nuns in brown and white habits moving about and heard some English being spoken in a completely foreign accent. I had never heard a broad Birmingham accent ever — let alone one tinged with provincial French, nor spoken to an eight year old little boy brought up in Belgium with a New Zealand father! I do not remember eating that evening, I can only remember the significance of the lock on the door.

Much later on I was in my room reading and there was comparative quiet, when I heard voices — German men's voices down below — a little rowdy — but it passed. Some minutes later I became aware of an odd noise. Shuffle - shuffle, pat pat, rattle rattle pause shuffle shuffle, pat tap, rattle rattle. Pause. It came nearer. It was next door! Silence. It started again. It was on my corridor wall! It stopped on the handle of my door which turned, was rattled once or twice, stopped, then continued down the corridor, eventually dying out. Now I could see why Papa insisted on the lock on my door! Had I not had one, the door would have opened and someone was on the other side.

I learnt more the next day … …

The proprietress of this 'hotel' was a certain Madame le Gros. She was an enormous fat lady, really enormous, who was in charge of the cooking for this motley group of French speaking foreigners dumped on her rather hastily by a German Officer. Her husband was a pathetic dirty unsavoury alcoholic who wandered over the place at night. The noisy crowd of soldiers had heard of the place, understood it to be the red light area of the small town — (several months before I learnt for the first time in France what a red light on a house signified) not knowing that the building had been requisitioned by the German occupying forces for the temporary internment of people like me!!

Chapter 5

Late Summer 1940

Part 2.

The following day we got organised. Madame Le Gros was relieved of all cooking and organising was taken over by a remarkable French woman whose daughter was with her, as was her eighty year old father Mr Lee (who was British) but who herself had been married at seventeen to a Canadian bear trapper!! She decided that all of us (forty approximately) who were fit, including 6 nuns from an exclusive Carmelite Order were to take it in turns — in 'teams' — to cook and wash up. She took it upon herself to pester the 'hotel proprietress' for our various needs and see the German Officer responsible if necessary. We were told that at 11 am each morning we were to report in the yard for a roll-call taken by a German to see that we were all there! After that we appeared to be free to come and go.

Papa arrived that morning. Evidently he had been very busy. By extraordinary circumstances he had met a man whose elderly 'Nanny' an English lady of sixty three, had been 'picked up' and moved to Carhaix where he had managed to get her into the cottage hospital as a 'patient'. He was Prince Poniatovski — had transport, a small useful van. It was his old family nanny in the hospital and I was asked by Papa to visit her of an afternoon

— and not to forget the flowers!! This I duly did and she was very sweet and pleased to see me. So Prince P. had the transport and Papa was bilingual German/French. Papa took away with him letters to friends and relations from our extraordinary group without of course the Germans knowing — and promised to return as soon as possible. Prince P's van was invaluable, for Papa's aim was to get in writing a permit to allow me out of the camp and to be moved far from the coast for apparently this was the German's fear — access to the U.K. by boat! He emphasised the point that I was only 18 (at that time 21 was the age of adulthood in both countries) and he was responsible for me. But where was the German hierarchy to sign such an undertaking? I know that Commandantur after Commandantur was visited and by fair means or foul at last the required piece of paper was obtained! This was the period when Hitler was at the peak of his confidence to invade Britain and all over the coastal roads in France cheeky wooden arrows pointed over the channel, to England —> à l'Angleterre —>. It was also the period when bodies, clad in German uniforms and badly burnt were being washed up on the coast and found on the beaches by French people.

After the war we learnt the truth. Flaming oil really was poured on the channel waters in those days approaching The Battle of Britain. The bodies washed up in the green uniforms had been the over-confident unsuspecting Germans attempting to cross the channel to invade Britain.

I was there two or three weeks, Papa coming quite often with news for other people as well as keeping up my morale. He was then absent for several days. The next time he came was about the first days in September. He was very brief. "Pack all your things together you are leaving tomorrow, I'll come and fetch you." I asked him where was I going. "I'll tell you when I see you," he replied. This caused a flutter in our community. What was going to happen to the others. The little nun Madeleine was going to Paris to her community — the others later were rumoured to have been taken to an internment camp in or near Switzerland. I never knew.

Chapter 6

a)   The Farm Girl

I had never worked on a farm before but as a teenager I had liked camping and open air activities. The large farm opposite was being run by a woman 'La Marthe' whose husband was one of the three million French prisoners and she was only too willing to have me as a help-mate and taught me the various jobs as the season progressed.

The harvest was followed by grape picking and wine making was in turn followed by white beet pulling and carrot silos. My sore hands toughened and I was well fed — eating always at the farm when I was working there.

One evening in early Spring 1941 Marthe said to me quietly before I went off "Come early tomorrow morning, about six, there is something we have to do. Don't mention it to anybody." I duly turned up, apart from cocks crowing the whole village was absolutely quiet. She was up. The horses were still in their stable, her two little boys and the old grandmother still in bed. She explained to me that it was rumoured that the Germans were requisitioning horses and oats. "They are not going to have mine", she said, "at least not the oats." She said that she and I were going to hide most of her oats (harvested that autumn and lying in a huge pile in one of the many storage barns) by shifting her winter log supply, putting the oats into sacks, replacing the wood by the sacks and restacking the wood against the sacks.

Just the two of us. She reckoned we would take most of the morning. Nobody was to know.

We set to work,. Log by log we moved from the back of the stone store the neatly piled logs — throwing them over to the other side. There were three or four rows of them. The wall was bare ready for our oats. Back we went to the huge heap of grain — this had to be put into smallish sacks and tied and trolleyed into the wood store. There, one by one, the sacks were set up against the wall as high as possible — two or three rows of these. We then set to, to put back in front of them the cut wood, in neat rows, so that it was very difficult indeed to see anything odd about the wood store. Three packed rows of wood going up higher than the oats behind them to an unsuspecting German Officer who with luck could have been from a town and knew nothing much about farming was we felt a safe bet. It worked. Nobody came that day. Nothing was said. Some time later she did have to part with one of the horses. The old grandmother was in a terrible state. She appeared to be more distressed about this horse than the fact that her son-in-law was a prisoner of war and not at home on the farm!

b)   Washing in the village

I have unhooked large frozen sheets from a washing line in an attic, and from a line in a barn, so stiff they were impossible to fold — but the day our precious piece of soap from the top of the washing tub slid all the way down a frozen path into the bushes, and had to be found, was no joke.

The household washing in winter, when the family were elsewhere, was done by a young Polish woman 'la Cata' — in the open lavoir below us at the bottom of a steep hill. In this open but roofed washhouse was fresh running water. We would fetch the washing up when finished, slowly and carefully, holding each side of the deep metal container ('la lessiveuse) the cold wet linen folded neatly with the precious bar of soap (if any remained) lying on the top. One morning, half way up, the soap slid off and down the hill it went bumping along the path to the bottom. We had to retrieve it! Soap was too precious, and was rationed — sold in three inch cube blocks the same soap for washing clothes as for washing faces. We put the washing bucket down tilting it slightly with a stone underneath it so that the freshly washed linen would not tip out all over the muddy crumbling path. Down we went looking everywhere for a small piece of greeny-yellow soap amongst the greeny-yellow muddy stones that made the path. We could hear the women below chattering, and one seemed to be shouting — she had seen from afar that we had stopped and were returning. At the bottom were clumps of nettles and other weeds. Finally in a small puddle we spotted our prize. We picked it up, called out to the sympathetic woman, turned back up the path — put the soap in one of our pockets and retrieved our washing. The upper part of the path was steeper and narrower and came out onto the rough lane by the side of our house. What a labour of love it was to keep clean!

While we were still warm we hung up the wet linen, stiffening already in the cold air, some in the attic, some in the barn. Pegs were not necessary, you hung the washing **over** the line, but the large heavy sheets needed two of us to handle them. There was enough linen in the house for this to be only a monthly chore, fortunately, so we could pick and choose the 'best' day and then hurry ourselves back into the warmest place — the large stone-floored kitchen with the old range fuelled by wood. A meal had to be cooked and Jacques and Yette looked after. Keeping clean in a very cold climate was quite demanding.

c)   **Other characters.**

"La Cata" who did our heavy washing at Beaumont sur Vingeanne lived with her little child in a small cottage at the bottom of the hill not far from the "lavoir". It was the home of an old recluse known as "le Père Simon". One day on passing I saw him in his small garden and he looked up and nodded. He had evidently heard of the English girl "marooned" in the village, for to my surprise he stopped digging and leant on his spade. He was old or at least seemed it but wanted to talk. He hadnt any time for wars he told me. He had avoided being called up in the 1st world war by a simple device. He had taken the wood cleaver and chopped off three of his toes on the left foot and could not be accepted into the army! He was not worried about rationing because he only ate honey and garlic with his bread, there was milk in the village that Cata fetched and he grew other vegetables. He looked after her little boy while she worked.
    Monsieur Faulknet lived by himself in a small house with a tower very near our own house. It had railings around it and many weeds. I remember that he always wore a cloth cap, nodded a greeting if seen but kept himself to himself. My Madame Poinselin told me that he was a lonely soul, had come from the town but did not mix very well.
    One old lady, a Madam Voiset, had a son who had married a town's girl and they lived in a small cottage right next to our large, walled house - and right on top of a small manure heap replenished by one horse and I think only one cow. A new baby had recently arrived and the "fils voiset" was renowned for always being at least two or three hours behind schedule - he would be just leaving the village for work when the others would be eating their "dixheures" (10 o"clock snack)

and would return home when dusk had long fallen. The new baby that I saw once was robustly swaddled and changed rarely - but it survived! Years later I learnt that his wife plus child left him in the village with his various chattels and returned with her son to the town where she did well for them both.

    The old lady Voiset worked for days at any of the large farms, potato gathering, grape picking, any of the seasonal jobs that were available. Her very small cottage into which she invited me one day to show me something consisted of a table in the middle of a grubby stone floor, a chicken tied to the leg of the table, and a huge old country bed in the corner with a massive duvet like the one in the corner of la Marthe's kitchen (where her mother in law slept). Swimming in the warm canal was a Summer activity we enjoyed whenever possible - German occupation or not - and to get to the canal we cut down through the woods passed the Père Simon's cottage, through the meadows where "colchique" crocuses pushed their way and up on to the flat canal bank. We had an enormous rubber innertube that we took it in turns to carry round our shoulders and served as a safety belt as well as a huge water toy when once at the canal. One day to our surprise a young man appeared on a bicycle on the other side and stopped to watch three young maidens and two small children having great fun in the warm water. He said he was staying in Fontainebleau - the small country town that we visited from time to time. He posed his bike, stripped down to his underpants, dived in and joined in the fun. He was obviously a "townie", helped Jacques and Yette to swim and was generally very pleasant company. He suddenly said "oh help"! I'll be missed I'd better be off, scrambled out (the only "muddy bit" of the sport) dressed quickly and with a quick wave and a thankyou for a pleasant afternoon disappeared down the towpath towards Fontainebleau.

A few days later I was invited by Monsieur le Marquis et Madame Marquise of Fontainebleau to lunch! They had heard on the pipeline of the English young lady "entrapped" in this adjacent village and either by curiosity or "politesse" wanted to see me! As a change from farm-house dining I accepted the invitation, though how I travelled there I do not remember. To my surprise there was a background presence of German Officers who clicked their heels and bowed with a "Hail Hitler" as usual and the Marquis explained that the Germans had requisitioned the chateau but had apportioned a small corner to the owners if they needed it. As we assembled for the meal I saw to my surprise the young man of the canal episode. He passed by sufficiently near to whisper quickly "please, you don't know me, we have not met". The meal was pleasant, semi formal - the inevitable chicken was served (there were two meals) but to my embarrassment the Marquis reprimanded her son for picking up his chicken to enjoy the meat on the bones (such as I had been doing many times in la Marthe's kitchen after the day's labour) and apologised to me as though I were shocked to the core! I saw no more of the young châtelain but often wondered what had happened to him.

Chapter 7

"Two lemons and five lumps of sugar"

It was half past six, quite dark, very cold. A little light filtered through the closed slatted shutters. The children were still asleep. No need to wake them up for another few minutes. I could hear noises from the outside world; some feet clattering, wooden soles on a cobbled street; a call of "Bonjour François, ca va?"; something falling and a muffled curse. Our house literally backed on to a sloping street with no windows or doors on that side at all. I cannot remember ever passing that way.

There were movements down below. That would be Denise a young daily help getting the small kitchen range going, having damped it down for the night. It provided a hot drink before going off to school. Must leave at a quarter to eight.

I crept out of bed in my thick striped men's pyjamas, slipped to the window, opened it with its central locking knob, pulling it inwards, pushed the wooden shutters right open and leant out, first left then right to clip them fast against the wall, before hastily retreating inside the room to close the windows to keep in the little warmth there was.

Then I remembered — it was my birthday! My 21st. We always recognised birthdays in the French family some way or another, not by candles on a cake and blowing them out and counting, but something special to eat as a dessert if it were possible, like a shop-made fruit flan from the baker's. But in war-time France, February 1943, we had a problem. We lived in the occupied zone. There was very strict rationing which included bread, sugar, jam and meat. In a kilo of sugar, always sold in lumps in oblong boxes there were about 180 pieces. Divide that into people per day it came to about 3. The problem was how to share it fairly. Keep some back and use it for stewing fruit? Make some sort of hot drink in cold weather? Suck it like a sweet? Crunch it with dry bread? (quite tasty if you are hungry). Who was to decide? The children were from six to seventeen years old and there were three adults.

Enough of this. A cold morning was breaking and it was getting lighter. Everyone had to get up, get off to school. I had shopping to do and the children must not be late. Jacques aged $7\frac{1}{2}$ and Yette aged 6 were stirring. We washed, dressed and dashed along the corridor past the older children's rooms down the uncarpeted wooden stairs into the living-dining room. Had we got our school books? Had we done our homework? What was the time? The children ate the small chunk of rationed bread, drank their hot milk, put on their thick winter capes with warm hoods and went out into the cold.

We had to cross a small icy garden — through a front gate, and then begin to join the growing stream of children and parents on their way to Primary school.

I had no time to think of 21st birthdays or anything else other than the immediate needs. We had a walk of about 10 minutes — Jacques and Yette were safe and sound until the midday pick-up — home for a meal — back to school at 2 until 4.30.

I walked briskly back to an emptying house (the older children were getting themselves off to school), past the little grocer's shop where I had placed some of the family's ration books, rounded the steep corner of the shoe maker's and went back up the street to the small garden gate. Langres was an ancient fortified town built on the remains of a volcano so was surrounded by high walls with huge old gates that during that period were open and closed by the German occupying forces and on which were fixed innumerable notices of DO's and DONT's, the most common word always being "Verboten" (forbidden).

At our garden gate I was stopped. The postman was just about to put into our metal letterbox a small packet addressed to me. "For me?" I thought, "that's odd." It was from Emma, seven years older than I was, not living at home any longer. I hurried in, up to my room, opened the packet and there on a small piece of paper was a brief note — "for your 21st — thought you would like these" — and in a small box were cushioned two real lemons and five lumps of sugar! I had not seen a lemon for more than three years and as for the sugar ......! My dear Emma had sent me this surprise for my 21st birthday.

At the end of afternoon school — the Primary schools finished earlier than the secondary schools — Jacques, Yette and I had our treat — three large thick dry 'Petain' biscuits washed down with delicious real lemonade made with real fruit and real sugar, a truly splendid refreshing celebration.

Note:-

Pétain biscuits resembled thick dog biscuits about 3 inches square called after Maréchal Petain and distributed by schools now and again direct to pupils according to the age of the children — to supplement the official poor diet. They would bring some home to me sometimes, when they had 'spares.'

Chapter 8

The Precious Tongue

Meat was severely rationed in occupied France — but not in the same way as in England. When the butcher **did** have some meat, he would put a notice in his window, and his regular customers took their turn.
You could then buy by weight your ration, $^1/_2$lb per person per week, for example, so if you wished to have an expensive cut with six books you could obtain 3lbs of steak or neck of lamb or sirloin — if there were any!!

One Saturday morning I went early to the butcher's hoping for something. When it was my turn the butcher put his head under the counter, took out a small parcel, handed it to me and said, "Here you are Mademoiselle, this will make a change for your family."

I paid him, left the shop, hurried home and opened up. It was a large cooked tongue, about ten inches long complete with skin. "That will do nicely for the evening meal this Sunday" I thought, "a pleasant surprise for everybody." I took it down to the small cool cellar under the house and put it away in the meat safe, a three-shelved aerated cupboard where we kept fresh cheese and other dairy products when we had them.

Sunday was a fine day, a good opportunity for a long walk in the nearby countryside (we were living at Langres at the time) and seven of us took a snack with us, stretched our legs and spent a pleasant day out. We arrived back about six o'clock. The children needed a break. I was going to prepare the evening meal — with the surprise cold tongue and salad, quick and easy to do.

I went down to the food safe in the cellar. The hinged door was slightly ajar. No sign of the tongue on the oval serving plate, but in its place our small dark cat Nounouche. Full with the helpings from the tongue, almost unable to move, he lay there half exhausted. I like cats normally, but on this occasion my feelings were very mixed! The aroused cat leapt out revealing the tongue with the tip gnored off and bits of skin hanging from it. I took plate and tongue out carefully, shut the food safe door, retraced my steps up to the small kitchen and looked at the disaster.

No way was I **not** going to produce an evening meal — in fact there was a sizeable piece of tongue left. I washed the ragged lump carefully in cold water, patted it dry in an old teatowel and started my handiwork. I cut off all the skin, removed the remains of the chewed end, took a spotlessly clean serving dish and started. Carefully cutting in thin strips little by little, from the new end of the tongue I produced enough thin slices for all the family to enjoy, garnishing here and there the circular pattern with fresh parsley sprigs I kept in a jar.

The meal was thoroughly enjoyed that evening. Madame who appeared at 7.30pm remarked on the happy atmosphere and hoped that we were all prepared for school the next day. Well fed and comfortably tired we wound down to bed-time.

No one knew the story of the tongue except Nounouche and me. That secret was kept for years, in fact I am probably the only one along with you dear Reader who knows it now.

Chapter 9

1944 My 5th Year

As the Spring of 1944 approached the war was changing shape and affecting us in many different ways. Monsieur had been appointed the regional Minister of Education and Sport in the Langres/Auxerre zone of occupied France and Madame had become Headmistress of the 'College de Jeunes Filles' at Langres. The boys' college building had to be used for the girls as well, boys attending in the morning, girls in the afternoon because the Germans had requisitioned the girls' school for their administrative purposes.

The general population minus most of its men had adapted itself to all kinds of changes, as had indeed the English population. In France there were virtually no shops to speak of. Apart from food there were few goods to buy or sell. One week an uncle in the North near Lille sent us five pairs of real leather boots. Excitedly we tried them on for size! To my joy I became the proud owner of a pair which I wore with thick boys' socks over thinner stockings whenever I went out.

As there were no clothes shops in Langres when a garment finally wore out to shreds, I would unpick very carefully a seam or hem, not cutting but keeping the thread, wound on to an empty cotton reel for further use! That was the true meaning of thrift!

No wonder I became a hoarder, unable to throw anything away — it might come in useful!

The R.A.F. were bombing railways and bridges all over the occupied zone, especially in Dijon a large provincial town where Emma now worked as a Social Worker. Our big house in Beaumont-sur-Vingeanne had been occupied by German army remnants over the winter of 1942-43 who had so badly damaged it that Madame Schlemmer insisted on a sulphur container being burned for three days in every room to disinfect the house which she said was infested by lice and bugs; it had been very cold and some of the thick parquet block-flooring had been prized out by the soldiers to fuel the stoves.

In March 1944 I returned to this house, with Yette, Jacques and Philippe, for school in Langres was barely functioning, to a house with its large stone floored kitchen, a wood fuelled iron stove like a large Aga, but to a house with no electricity supply. That meant no lights and no working water pump.

News of what was happening in the outside world was obtained from a nearby miller who, because of his water-well, had a working radio! "Ici Londres, ici Londres" every evening at the same time. "Ici le bulletin d'information français". Somebody went from the village and returned with snippets of news. But this was not only news for us. There were many Resistance groups functioning in the region and we could hear the messages being sent to them.

"The white rabbits are in the field, repeat, the white rabbits are in the field." "The garden is muddy today, repeat, the garden is muddy today, repeat, the garden is muddy today."

These coded messages (there would be twelve or more) conveyed to the Resistance groups in the area a variety of things. At Langres, I learnt later the Resistance group in the town was made up of the part-time fire brigade, complete with fire-engines that carried their own water. At 7 a.m. on certain mornings with much noise of ringing bells, several engines would speed out through the huge iron town gates opened by the Germans, down the hill into the countryside, up another hill into far off thick forests to the 'fire'. They would return several hours later, their water tanks emptied and refilled with small arms or radio equipment that had been dropped by the R.A.F. in the dark. I was told this by a retired fireman several years later. The Germans 'guarding' Langres never found out.

Chapter 10

The Beginning of the End ………

Emma in Dijon had a 5 month old daughter Catherine. The town was being bombed by the R.A.F. and parents were ordered to evacuate all children overnight. Dijon was an important railway junction, an escape route for Germans fleeing eastwards. The population were entrapped by those liberating them and those occupying them! So we were joined in Beaumont by baby Catherine for whom I became responsible and her mother came down to see her whenever possible. Little Catherine blossomed with plenty of attention — she is now 59 years old, has three children of her own and we have kept in touch!!

Fortunately we had some light in the form of candles which were kept strictly for evening or night use. Over the last two years we had learnt the art of bottling peas in champagne bottles with wired corks, of storing barrels of green beans in layers of salt and, of course, shelling beans at the end of the season to store away dried haricot beans for winter meals. From a friendly elderly bee-keeper in the next village we obtained honey for a treat, well worth the 5 kilometre tramped to fetch it in an enormous green glass container — all carried by hand on a pole contraption that we had invented. We never had enough potatoes, so with baby Catherine on my arm I would tramp round to friendly farms trying to buy a few kilos here and there only to be refused quite seriously on several occasions that they were very sorry but they had not sufficient for their pigs! We did at least have the offer of fresh white cheese, and from our own garden fresh vegetable soup. We had as well plenty of milk from the cows opposite (rice pudding!) and sometimes a huge round farmhouse loaf baked in the farm kitchen oven — otherwise we only had the very meagre bread ration. The occasional egg was available, but not often, and with at least seven mouths to feed an 'occasional' egg did not go very far!

We did not know much about the Normandy landings but became aware of happenings around Paris. Rumours were rife and strangers would occasionally pass through on motor cycles. The little village café became the source of information — all news was spread by word of mouth.

One evening at the beginning of September four or five French speaking soldiers came, I believe they were Belgians, telling us all (there were not many people in the village, only women, old men and children) to keep a low profile if any Germans came through and to let them have any bicycles they wanted because they were fleeing back eastwards. Some in fact were entrapped both in the S.W. of France and later in Belgium in the Ardennes in the famous Battle of the Bulge. At this time (September 1944) this had not occurred — it happened to American Troops in Christmas 1944 after I had arrived in England but by an extraordinary coincidence to the very same American soldiers that I had met in Langres in October 1944 who had moved on eastwards and to Bastogne.

One morning a few days later, about the 5th September, I was awakened by a loud rumbling sound — nothing else — going through the village on what we called the top road (this was the main road from Dijon to Fontaine Française). I quickly slipped on some clothes and crept out — without shoes in my excitement and saw at the end of a side path lorries and other vehicles going by. Something was stirring! It was from about this time I think that I began to live on a high. After five years I had stopped thinking of returning home to England. My French family especially the children had become my everyday life. I was in fact the 12th child as my French maman remarked one day! The four eldest had left home and I had become the remaining oldest one with six younger ones for whom I was very responsible.

On September 11 1944, early evening, more soldiers on motorbikes came into the village. They came up from the south. We were liberated they told us!

Some Resistance groups were nearby (all young men late teens, early twenties) and we benefited from their actions. They had blown up lock gates on the main canal just below the village (France was and is still riddled with hundreds of canals) carrying barges of sugar. The Resistance had 'requisitioned' the barges and their contents, unable to move as the unusable lock gates barred their passage. They coolly, with much boisterous humour, distributed the sugar to all nearby villages, 8 kilos of sugar per person — free! This meant for our family 7 x 8 = 56 kilos. I spent hours making jam in the large kitchen on my old-fashioned wood-fuelled stove with these young men unshaven from the woods wiping out the jam pan and dancing madly on the heavy old wooden kitchen table, waving wooden spoons and singing rowdily.

Martha in the farm opposite cleared one of her huge barns and we had an evening 'Do' before the boys moved on — dancing and singing and generally celebrating. The girls sang their student songs and the young men responded with more. I was 22 years of age and swapped a big square headscarf with that of one of the young men of the Resistance — his was a large torn off corner of an orange parachute, grubby and oily; I have kept it to this day. I have another souvenir. Claude, aged 20, had made me a blue voile party dress.

We had kept from Morlaix some curtains used in one of the bedrooms — and just like Scarlet O'Hara in 'Gone with the Wind' (Margaret Mitchell's racy romantic novel of the American Civil War that we had all read) Claude made me a beautiful full skirted blue dress with puffed up sleeves for the occasion! I have also to this day the skirt of this dress. The blue voile has **not** rotted!

The young men left the village. We had to go back to Langres. Baby Catherine was returned to Dijon. School had to begin again.

I had not heard from my home for many months. The only means of travel was by old vehicles on poor roads, half of which were badly damaged. And all the bridges spanning the main rivers were blown up. There were no trains. Americans in small companies here and there occupied the German commandanturs — offices left empty overnight as Germans fled eastward.

I do not remember how we returned to Langres — but we did, and found an American company had taken over the old German occupied premises. I was of course completely absorbed into my French family but as far as the American administration was concerned I was non-existent. The last person an American soldier expected to find was an English-speaking young woman in occupied France. I had had no news from England, the telegrams via Switzerland had ceased.

One morning having taken Jacques and Yette to school I passed by an American soldier standing at attention outside a doorway leading up to offices used by Americans, taken over from the Germans. I stopped. "May I speak to your Officer please" — not knowing what rank Officer was in charge of this unit. The young soldier nearly fell over hearing an English voice.

He took me up the narrow stairs into a room where there was jocular talk and I was ushered into a small office where a large American told me to sit down — not believing his eyes either!

He questioned me over this and that, I was finding it difficult to speak in English which to them was a little strange. I asked him whether he knew how I could get to Paris, which I knew was liberated, because I had to get home! He said he would look into it because road travel was difficult. I evidently sowed some ideas for two or three days later they told me that three of them had had permission to go to Paris in a jeep and would take me to the British Consulate which we thought would have been re-established, and might be able to help me (I had never lost my precious passport of 1939). The War of course was not over, there were German troops still in France and people who had collaborated (called 'les collaborateurs') were despised and taunted. (This occurred with the daughters in the famous 'Michelin' confectioners and Mustard Manufacturers in Dijon who had traded with the Germans. They were publicly head-shaved and ridiculed in the streets of Dijon). My French family were excited for me and I was facing up to the fact that I was leaving the children and all we shared.

Early one morning I found myself travelling with an overnight bag and three Americans who looked upon this journey as an adventurous jaunt — they wanted to visit Paris (partly damaged but not badly so, and I needed help to return home). I found the re-established British Embassy building and astounded a gentleman, who was the acting Ambassador I presumed, on presenting myself. "Where on earth have you come from" he said. "We have spent a few weeks rehabilitating English Nationals by 'plane on a daily basis. There will be no aeroplanes until Sunday week, November 19th. I suggest you go back to your French family and make your preparations. There is, I believe, a small postal van that goes each morning from the main post office yard, which takes odd passengers if it's urgent."

My American 'friends' were wanting to stay in Paris. They suggested that I got myself to the nearest town to Langres where I might get another lift and prepare for a journey to England! I stayed the night in a very grotty little boarding house and found the post office van in the morning. The driver kindly offered to take me with 3 other passengers. Two were an elderly couple wanting to visit long lost relations somewhere near Dijon and shared some fresh bread with us. The third was a new experience for me. He was an artistic character from Montmartre, he told us. He survived on the edge of things, and glad of what he felt was a captive audience (we were in the back of an enclosed van) he recounted stories of pre-war Paris when every month in the Montmartre quarter, where artists painted in the open air (and still do), their completely bare models displayed their charms without any inhibitions. I think that the elderly couple were bewildered to say the least and glad when they were dropped off! I was left with the unusual artist who fortunately alighted soon after. I remember his saying that he was hoping to look up some old acquaintance that he had known in the past. I wished him good luck and he went.

My post office driver kindly dropped me off where he thought an American unit might be, about 40 miles from Langres. I was lucky. Again I found some helpful drivers who could hardly believe what they were seeing, but who obligingly drove a very tired and hungry young English woman back to her family in Langres who were glad to see her, fed her and tucked her up for the night — that was when we stopped talking!

Chapter 11

The End

The following week in November 1944 went very quickly. The children were in and out of school, I had packing to do, treasures to take (like the children's drawings) and a large old trunk full of warm clothes less those on my back, for it was winter and very cold. We were all excited and yet upset. Who was going to do this now and arrange that, I had been doing the housekeeping accounts and shopping for some time. Promises of coming back soon once I knew my English family were alright and quite a few tears especially from Jacques (he was now $8\frac{1}{2}$ and had been taught to read by me). I did not know what to expect in my home town of Croydon.

We had a party for our American friends, who were moving on and once again I had to get to Paris for the 19th November. I do not remember how or where in Paris — I presume Orly Airport but I **do** remember the Dakota aircraft with an interior devoid of all comfort except — a type of safety belt (I was seated on bare metal) I remember other passengers, none of whom I knew, being air sick around me over the channel, with very noisy vibrating metal around us.

We landed at Croydon Airport — how fortunate for me, for I would be only a few miles away from my home. There was a very strict vetting of all passengers, I had my precious passport, but all luggage was retained except very small hand luggage which in my case was a little leather vanity case in which I stored all my 'correspondence' of the war. They didn't look into it but everything else was kept behind including, I remember, some perfectly innocent sheet music which I was informed could be coded!

It was getting dusk. People were met and drifted away. Once again I was left (shades of my first Thursday in France in 1939!). On looking around I saw a uniformed pilot who approached me. "You look lost, can I help[?" I told him that I lived in Croydon and that my parents had been informed two days previously that I might be arriving on that Sunday. (A primitive telegram system had started) "I've got a car here and I am going up to London. Let me take you home. I would like to. I wish I had a home to go to!" So he did.

Somehow we wended our way through empty Sunday streets that I was trying to recognise. On the outskirts of Addiscombe I saw buildings here and there that I had known, many bare spaces that I had not known but I was looking for 'The Black Horse' — a well known public house/small hotel that I hoped was still standing. It was, very dimly lit for black-out restrictions were still in force. I knew I was only a stone's throw away, but we had to wend our way round four turnings to No.6, Tenterden Rd. to a house that I had left in July 1939.

My parents were at the gate having spent almost the whole day on the look out. The airman just dropped me off, would not stay, and there I was! Hugs of course — we did not know what to say!

We went in. I was wearing my heavy warm boots from our uncle in the north. My mother was a little horrified but quickly said that it didn't matter about clothes or night clothes because we did not change, we were sleeping under the stairs not out in the dug-out shelter! Croydon had been receiving the doodlebugs — those slow moving pilotless air missiles that people tried to dodge! Only a little later the V2 rockets began to fall on London. In early Spring when the war had become very intense in parts of Belgium and France I was nearly obliterated near Holborn in London by a V2 which fell on a meat market mid-morning. To have survived $5^{1}/_{2}$ years in occupied France to being obliterated in England by a new kind of missile was not my idea of a joke!

I settled badly. Lovely to be back but empty and strange. I missed my family, the children and I expect the responsibility. My dear mother wanted to mother me all over again. I had no personal friends — they were either still in the forces or married to servicemen elsewhere. I wrote long letters to the girls in France, Monique especially. It was the end — but also the beginning. When I left that Sunday and Papa had managed to see me off he wished me emotionally "Bon Courage" and remarked that much as I had become involved with the family, time had a way of smoothing things out and in years to come I would probably forget my youthful exploits! I did not. I reminded him of this thirty years later when he was an old gentleman in his 80's!

My children have met their children. Our grandchildren know their grandchildren. It has been in fact another beginning.